ANCIENT
MESOPOTAMIA

BY MADELINE TYLER

KidHaven
PUBLISHING

UNLOCKING ANCIENT CIVILIZATIONS

Published in 2019 by KidHaven Publishing, an Imprint of Greenhaven Publishing, LLC
353 3rd Avenue, Suite 255, New York, NY 10010

© 2019 Booklife Publishing

This edition is published by arrangement with Booklife Publishing.

Written by: Madeline Tyler
Edited by: John Wood
Designed by: Daniel Scase

Cataloging-in-Publication Data

Names: Tyler, Madeline.
Title: Ancient Mesopotamia / Madeline Tyler.
Description: New York : KidHaven Publishing, 2019. | Series: Unlocking ancient civilizations | Includes glossary and index.
Identifiers: ISBN 9781534529113 (pbk.) | ISBN 9781534529137 (library bound) | ISBN 9781534529120 (6 pack) |
ISBN 9781534529144 (ebook)
Subjects: LCSH: Iraq--Civilization--To 634--Juvenile literature. | Iraq--Civilization--To 634--Juvenile literature.
Classification: LCC DS71.T95 2019 | DDC 935--dc23

Printed in the United States of America

CPSIA compliance information: Batch # BW19KL: For further information
contact Greenhaven Publishing LLC, New York, New York at 1-844-317-7404.

PHOTO CREDITS

ANCIENT
MESOPOTAMIA

CONTENTS

Words that look like *this* are explained in the glossary on page 31.

ANCIENT MESOPOTAMIA

THE FERTILE CRESCENT

MESOPOTAMIA was a region in the ancient world, in present-day Iraq. It was part of a larger area called the Fertile Crescent that stretches from Egypt to Iran and includes Iraq, Syria, Lebanon, Cyprus, Jordan, Palestine, Israel, and Turkey. The Nile, Euphrates, and Tigris rivers provided the Fertile Crescent with a supply of freshwater and made it the perfect place for *tribes* to settle and form *civilizations.* The freshwater from the rivers, the warm weather, and the *rich* soil made the area very *fertile* for growing crops.

THIS MAP SHOWS THE FERTILE CRESCENT. IT IS THE AREA SHADED IN RED.

TIGRIS RIVER

Some of the first civilizations in the world started in the Fertile Crescent. Most of them began as small tribes, but developed into large societies that were led by a king and followed set rules and laws. They were some of the first people to build cities, follow an *organized religion*, use a written language, and study subjects like science.

Mesopotamia was the area of land between the Tigris River and the Euphrates River. Many different people lived in Mesopotamia, and they all belonged to different tribes and civilizations. They spoke different languages, were ruled by different kings, and had different cultures. Mesopotamia is sometimes called the "cradle of civilization" because it is where human civilizations first began.

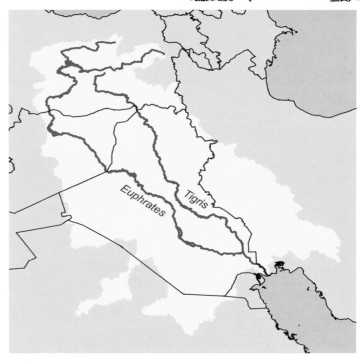

Many civilizations successfully grew and **thrived** in Mesopotamia by making use of the rivers and fertile land. They developed farming **communities** that grew lots of crops. Before this, tribes had to hunt for their food. Farming helped people to grow lots of food for the whole community.

They also tamed animals such as sheep and dogs, and kept them as pets or on farms to be used for food. They built cities that traded food and other goods with Europe, Egypt, and India. Three of the most important and **influential** civilizations that existed in Mesopotamia were Sumer, Assyria, and Babylonia.

THE WORD "MESOPOTAMIA" MEANS "BETWEEN TWO RIVERS".

SUMER

PEOPLE first settled in Sumer, in southern Mesopotamia, in around 5000 **B.C.** At first, they lived in small communities that farmed the land for food. The small villages and towns they built soon grew into cities and city-states. A city-state is a city that is like a small country – it is completely in charge of its own rules and laws, Each city-state had its own government and army, and they often went to war with each other. The Sumerian city-states were the first city-states in the world, and some of the most important cities were Uruk, Eridu, Larsa, Ur, Nippur, Adab, Kullah, Isin, Kish, and Lagash. Some historians believe that Uruk and Eridu were the world's first cities and that, at their largest, they may have had up to 80,000 people living in them.

RUINS OF A TEMPLE IN NIPPUR

RUINS OF URUK

Uruk was founded in around 4500 B.C. by the Sumerian king Enmerkar. Uruk is sometimes considered the first true city and is where both writing and stone structures like the ziggurat first appeared.

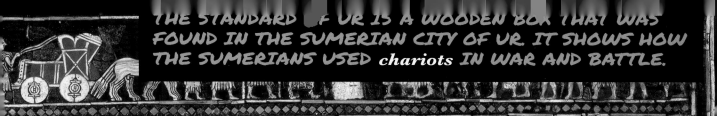

Many things began in Sumer that would later be used across Mesopotamia and the rest of the world. The Sumerians created number systems and a written language. They also used wheels to make chariots, and developed new methods for farming. These discoveries helped Sumer to develop very quickly and become a successful civilization. The Sumerian civilization thrived for thousands of years until around 2334 B.C. when it fell to the Akkadian Empire and later in 1750 B.C. when the Elamite and Amorite people invaded and moved into Sumer.

THIS *stele* WAS MADE IN AROUND 2250 B.C. TO CELEBRATE THE AKKADIAN KING NARAM-SIN AND THE BATTLE HE WON AGAINST A TRIBE OF PEOPLE CALLED THE LULLUBI.

Sargon of Akkad, or Sargon the Great, was the first emperor of the Akkadian Empire. The Akkadian Empire began in northern Mesopotamia but eventually spread to southern Mesopotamia, where the Akkadians *conquered* the Sumerians. He became the first leader to bring different areas of Mesopotamia together under one ruler.

ASSYRIA

ASSYRIA was a **kingdom** and an empire in Mesopotamia. The Assyrian Empire first began in around 1900 B.C. when its capital, Ashur, was founded after the Akkadian Empire ended. They had control over much of northern Mesopotamia and their power lasted for around 1,300 years.

AN ASSYRIAN WAR CHARIOT

Trade was very important in Mesopotamia and is one of the most important ways that Assyria was able to grow and extend its empire. Many **merchants** traveled to different cities from the capital, Ashur, to sell food and trade goods. The merchants also bought materials like iron to bring back to Ashur. The iron was then used to make weapons for Assyrian soldiers. The iron weapons were much stronger than the copper and tin weapons used by other armies in Mesopotamia. This helped the Assyrians to defeat their enemies and conquer other Mesopotamian people.

THE ASSYRIANS USED HORSES AND IRON WEAPONS TO CONQUER THEIR ENEMIES.

TIGLATH-PILESER III

Tiglath-Pileser III was a fierce warrior and was the ruler of Assyria in the 8th century B.C. He became king in around 745 B.C. after fighting in a *civil war* against Ashur-Nirari V, the previous king of Assyria. Tiglath-Pileser III made the Assyrian Empire even larger by conquering other civilizations such as Babylonia and Phoenicia. To show their strength and power, the Assyrians destroyed the city of Babylon, the capital of Babylonia, in 689 B.C. Tiglath-Pileser III's empire became known as the New Assyrian Empire and it lasted for over 100 years.

Although the Assyrians were powerful for many years, their empire eventually fell to the Medes and the Babylonians when Nineveh, their last city, was captured in 612 B.C. The Medes people were from a region called Media, and the Babylonians belonged to an empire called the Babylonian Empire. The Babylonians recaptured Babylon and conquered other civilizations to create a large empire that spread across Mesopotamia.

THIS *relief* FROM AROUND 695 B.C. WAS FOUND IN NINEVEH AND SHOWS A BULL HUNT.

MANY RELIEFS HAVE BEEN FOUND IN THE ANCIENT PALACE OF SARGON II, AN ASSYRIAN KING DURING THE 8TH CENTURY B.C. THIS ONE SHOWS SOME SERVANTS CARRYING A BENCH, A CHAIR, AND A VASE.

BABYLONIA
THE OLD BABYLONIAN EMPIRE

NEARLY 4,000 years ago, in the 18th century B.C., the Babylonians built an early civilization in southern Mesopotamia while the Assyrians were in control of the north. In around 1792 B.C., Hammurabi became king of Babylon, a city-state in Mesopotamia and the capital of Babylonia. Hammurabi led many wars against other nearby cities until eventually Babylon became the center of a very large empire that covered the whole of Mesopotamia.

HAMMURABI

Hammurabi was the king of Babylonia until 1750 B.C. While he was king, Hammurabi came up with a set of laws called the Code of Hammurabi. The Code of Hammurabi contained 282 different laws about money and trade, marriage and divorce, *assault*, and *slavery*. The laws told Mesopotamian people what they were and were not allowed to do, and what the punishments were for breaking any of the laws. The Code of Hammurabi was one of the first sets of laws in the world and many future laws in other countries were based on Hammurabi's code.

THE CODE OF HAMMURABI WAS WRITTEN ON
A LARGE STELE AND DISPLAYED IN A TEMPLE.

NEO-BABYLONIAN EMPIRE

RUINS OF BABYLON

In 1225 B.C., an Assyrian king called Tukulti-Ninurta I attacked Babylon and took control of the city. The Assyrians were very powerful and were in charge of Babylon and the Babylonian Empire for hundreds of years. However, in 612 B.C. the Babylonians and the Medes people captured the Assyrian city of Nineveh, and Babylon became the most powerful city in Mesopotamia.

NEBUCHADNEZZAR II

Nebuchadnezzar II was the king of Babylon from 605 B.C. until 562 B.C. He helped Babylonia to become a powerful and thriving empire again by fighting his enemies for new lands. Nebuchadnezzar II spent many years rebuilding Babylon to make it a great city again after lots of it was destroyed by the Assyrians. He built a large palace and several temples for the gods. Babylon soon became one of the greatest cities in the world for art and education and had some of the grandest buildings in Mesopotamia.

The Babylonians ruled their empire from the city of Babylon. The Old Babylonian Empire began in the 18th century B.C. and lasted until they were defeated by a group called the Hittites. The Neo-Babylonian Empire began hundreds of years later in the 6th century B.C. During this time, new buildings and city walls were added to Babylon to make sure that it was strong enough to keep enemies and invaders out.

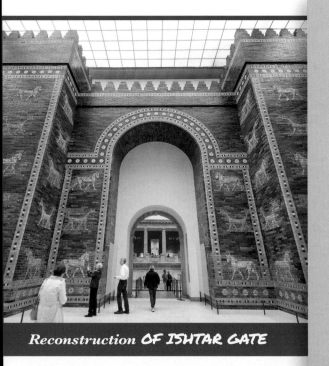

Reconstruction OF ISHTAR GATE

The first walls surrounding Babylon were built by Hammurabi after 1792 B.C., but Nebuchadnezzar II added to them while he was king. He built three huge walls to surround Babylon that were over 39 feet (12 m) tall. Some ancient writers and historians said that the walls were over 56 miles (90 km) long, 79 feet (24 m) thick, and 318 feet (97 m) high, although no one is sure if this is true.

There were many gates within the city walls that allowed people to enter and leave Babylon. Ishtar Gate was the main entrance into Babylon and was built by Nebuchadnezzar II in around 575 B.C.

ZIGGURATS

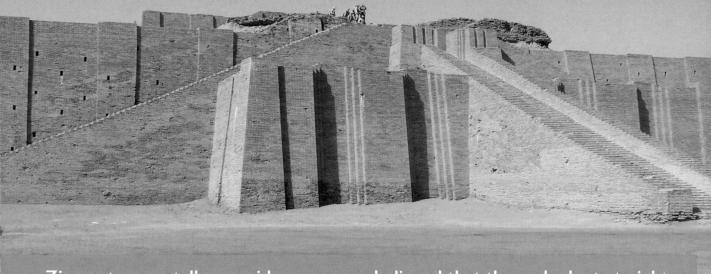

Ziggurats were tall pyramids that could be found throughout Mesopotamia, usually at the center of a city. They had levels at different heights that had stairs in between them. They had a temple at the top where the Mesopotamian people believed that the gods slept at night. The ziggurats were built very high so that the temple could be as close to the heavens as possible. The first ziggurats in Mesopotamia were built over 4,000 years ago in the Sumerian city of Ur.

In the center of Babylon there was a pyramid called the Etemenanki Ziggurat. It was a huge temple dedicated to Marduk, the Mesopotamian god of Babylon. Like other ziggurats, it was made by sticking mud bricks together with more mud. Some historians believe that this ziggurat was 295 feet (90 m) tall, although they do not know this for sure because only the foundations survive today.

MUD BRICK

THE HANGING GARDENS OF BABYLON

THE HANGING GARDENS OF BABYLON ARE ONLY A *legend*. NO RUINS OR EVIDENCE OF THE GARDENS HAVE EVER BEEN FOUND, SO NO ONE KNOWS FOR SURE IF THEY EXISTED OR NOT.

THE Hanging Gardens of Babylon was a legendary structure said to have been built sometime during the **reign** of Nebuchadnezzar II. Some people believe that Nebuchadnezzar II had the Hanging Gardens built for his wife, Amytis. Queen Amytis was from Media, a region in present-day Iran. Media had many mountains and lots of greenery, so Nebuchadnezzar II hoped that the Hanging Gardens of Babylon would remind Amytis of her home and make her feel less homesick in the very flat and dry desert of Babylon.

Some historians have suggested a theory that the Hanging Gardens may have instead been built by an Assyrian king called Sennacherib around 100 years before Nebuchadnezzar II's rule, in Nineveh. Historians believe they were sloping to look like a real mountain.

The Hanging Gardens of Babylon would have been built on a large ziggurat pyramid on several different levels, close to the royal palace in Babylon. Almond, olive, plum, pear, fig trees, and grapevines all grew in Babylonia, so it is likely that they were planted at the Hanging Gardens. The ziggurat would have been made of baked mud bricks and surrounded by canals. The canals brought water from the Euphrates River and watered the plants, while the mud bricks kept the ziggurat from getting too dry.

The Hanging Gardens of Babylon is one of the Seven Wonders of the Ancient World. This is a collection of buildings and structures built by the earliest civilizations that are considered some of the best examples of human skill and creativity. Possibly the most famous structure on this list is the Great Pyramid of Giza, built by the ancient Egyptians over 4,000 years ago.

GREAT PYRAMID OF GIZA, EGYPT

EVERYDAY LIFE

SOCIAL CLASSES

Mesopotamian society had a *hierarchy* with different *social classes*. The king and his family were at the very top. The king ruled over his region and Mesopotamian people believed that he was closer to the gods than anyone else.

Priests and priestesses were just below the royalty. They led religious *ceremonies* and told people how to behave in order to please the gods. Many priestesses were also doctors and healers, and helped people who were sick. Priests had shaved heads so that people could easily recognize them.

Mesopotamian people loved music, dancing, and storytelling. They played instruments like drums, flutes, and harps during festivals. Storytellers passed down stories to their children and grandchildren until they started to be written down on clay tablets.

Scribes, tutors, and other educated people were part of the upper class, while the lower class was made up of people like farmers, brickmakers, butchers, and fishermen.

Slaves were part of the lowest social class. They were usually captured in a war and bought by the king, priests, or members of the upper class.

STORIES AND POEMS WERE WRITTEN ON CLAY TABLETS LIKE THIS ONE.

LIVING IN A MESOPOTAMIAN CITY

Homes in Sumer and Babylonia were very similar. The houses were grouped around the ziggurat in the center of the city. They were built from sandstone and mud bricks and were usually three stories high. The roof was always flat so that it could be used as a fourth floor in nice weather. Rich people of the upper class had wide houses while people of the lower class had narrow houses and would often share walls with other houses to make building them cheaper.

In Babylon, people threw their trash into the street from their front door. This made the city very dirty. The street would sometimes get covered with a new layer of clay to cover the trash and make it level again.

RESTORED RUINS OF BABYLON

Assyrian homes were built from stone, not sandstone or mud bricks. Their flat roofs were covered in a thick layer of earth. This kept the homes *insulated* and also made them fireproof. These homes were much more *permanent* than the ones in Babylonia or Sumer.

RELIGION

GODS

RELIGION was very important to Mesopotamian people, and they had a god for almost every aspect of daily life. Every god had a specific job and they were worshipped almost every day.

The Sumerian people had hundreds of gods. Some gods were dedicated to a specific city, while others were the chosen god of a *profession* like fishing or building. Each person had their own personal god that looked after them. They worshipped this god and tried to live their life in a way that would please them. Sumerians believed that good things would happen if they pleased the gods, and bad things were the result of making them angry. Although a lot of time was spent praying to their personal god, all Sumerian gods were as important as each other and Sumerian people wanted to please all of them.

The Babylonians and Assyrians worshipped many of the same gods as the Sumerians. They based their religions on Sumerian gods and beliefs, and added their own gods, too.

SUMERIAN GODS AND GODDESSES INANNA, UTU, ENKI, AND ISIMUD

The Babylonians believed that some gods were more important than others. The most important Babylonian god was Marduk, the god of Babylon. Marduk was above all other Babylonian gods and had up to 50 different names. Another important Babylonian god was Nergal, the god of the underworld. Some Babylonians believed that Nergal was evil and brought war and hunger to them, while others believed that he could bring people back to life and protected their animals and crops.

MARDUK IS OFTEN REPRESENTED BY MUŠHUŠŠU, A MYTHICAL DRAGON WITH A HORNED HEAD AND A SNAKE'S TONGUE.

THE HEAD OF THE ASSYRIAN GODS WAS ASHUR, GOD OF WAR. ASSYRIANS PRAYED TO ASHUR AND ASKED HIM TO HELP THEM WIN THEIR BATTLES AGAINST ENEMIES.

Mesopotamians worshipped their gods at the temples in their cities. The temples were built on top of large ziggurats in an effort to make them closer to the gods. Every city in Mesopotamia had at least one ziggurat temple. Priests studied the stars and planets and led religious rituals from the temples.

LANGUAGE AND WRITING

SUMERIAN language and writing first appeared in Mesopotamia in around 3100 B.C. and was the main spoken language for around 1,000 years, until it was replaced by Akkadian. Akkadian was used by the Assyrians in northern Mesopotamia and the Babylonians in southern Mesopotamia. However, even when Akkadian overtook Sumerian to become the most widely spoken language, Sumerian was still used in writing for many years after.

The Sumerians were the first people in the world to develop a writing system. At first, they used pictures to represent different words, but they eventually began using a new system called cuneiform. Cuneiform involved small, wedge-shaped symbols that were used to represent different sounds and meanings. Sumerians, Akkadians, Babylonians, Assyrians, and all other Mesopotamian civilizations used cuneiform until sometime after 100 B.C. when they began using letters of the alphabet instead.

AKKADIAN CUNEIFORM SCRIPT

THE EPIC TALE OF GILGAMESH
WRITTEN ON A CLAY TABLET

Writing developed in Sumer because the people needed a way of recording everything that happened in the growing civilization. The Sumerians needed to keep track of important things like the sale and trade of different products and the names of different rulers. They also wrote myths, songs, and poems about Mesopotamian gods and heroes. Not many people in Mesopotamia knew how to write. People called scribes received special training that taught them how to write Sumerian and Akkadian using cuneiform. Scribes were usually upper-class boys or men.

The most famous Sumerian story is the Epic Tale of Gilgamesh. It was first recorded onto tablets in around 2000 B.C. by a scribe. It is about someone called Gilgamesh who is part human and part god. Gilgamesh is the king of Uruk and is the strongest and most powerful man in the world. The gods send Gilgamesh a wild man called Enkidu to test his power and strength, but they eventually became best friends.

STATUE OF GILGAMESH

ART AND CULTURE

ARTISTS and craftspeople were very important in all civilizations of Mesopotamia. They made lots of useful things such as clay tablets, weapons, tools, and chariots. Some people called potters made pots out of clay that could be used to store food and water in. They developed a special wheel that could be used to make pots more quickly and learned that baking clay caused it to harden. Sumerian pottery was so valuable that they used it instead of money, trading it for things like food.

GOLD HAIR ACCESSORIES

Jewelers made necklaces, earrings, and bracelets using gold, silver, and gemstones. Men and women both wore jewelry, but only royalty and the upper class wore the best pieces. There were also metalworkers, or metalsmiths, that made bronze by mixing two metals called tin and copper together. They used the bronze to make weapons for war, and sculptures of their gods and kings.

Stonemasons carved sculptures from stone. A sculpture is a piece of art that is usually made out of a hard material. Unlike drawings or paintings, sculptures are usually objects such as statues and figures. The sculptures made by stonemasons in Mesopotamia were kept in temples and were often religious, representing either a god or a king. Mesopotamian people could present *offerings* to them in the temples during ceremonies or other special religious days.

STATUES OF GUDEA

The statues of Gudea are a collection of around 27 statues that were made in southern Mesopotamia. They were carved around 4,000 years ago and were made to represent the Mesopotamian ruler Gudea during his reign. Gudea was ruler of the Sumerian city Lagash between 2144 and 2124 B.C. Most of the statues were made from stones called dolomite and diorite. Dolomite and diorite are very hard types of stone, which helped the statues to survive for such a long time.

THE END OF ANCIENT MESOPOTAMIA

CYRUS THE GREAT

THERE were several different causes that led to the collapse of ancient Mesopotamia and its many civilizations, but the main one was invasion and war. In 550 B.C., a leader called Cyrus the Great rose to power and became the emperor of the Achaemenid Empire (also known as the First Persian Empire). Cyrus conquered Babylon in 539 B.C. and defeated the Neo-Babylonian Empire. The Achaemenid Empire soon grew to include Egypt, Israel, and Turkey, as well as Mesopotamia. It stretched around 3,100 miles (5,000 km) and was the largest empire on Earth at the time. At its height, 44% of the world's population were under the control of the Achaemenid Empire.

In 485 B.C., Cyrus's grandson and the new ruler of the Achaemenid Empire, Xerxes I, destroyed Babylon to stop a rebellion. He destroyed the temples and melted down the golden statue of Marduk, the god of Babylon.

THIS IS THE GATE OF XERXES IN THE ANCIENT CITY OF PERSEPOLIS, IRAN. IT WAS BUILT BY, AND IS NAMED AFTER, XERXES I.

ALEXANDER THE GREAT

Hundreds of years later, in 333 B.C., a man called Alexander the Great conquered the Achaemenid Empire and expanded his own empire. Alexander the Great was the king of Macedonia and ruler of a large empire from 336 B.C. until his death in 323 B.C. After defeating the Persians, Alexander the Great led his army to India, leaving a Greek *governor* in every new place that he conquered.

THIS MAP SHOWS THE DIFFERENT EMPIRES IN 336 B.C. WHEN ALEXANDER THE GREAT BECAME KING OF MACEDONIA.

In 651 *A.D.*, the remaining parts of Mesopotamia were controlled by the Sasanian Empire, which was ruled by King Yazdegerd III. However, it was around this time that Muslim Arabs arrived and overthrew the Sasanian Empire. During this time, any remains of Mesopotamian culture were destroyed when the Muslim Arabs brought their own law, language, and religion of Islam into the area.

THESE COINS SHOW IMAGES OF KING YAZDEGERD III DURING HIS LAST YEAR ON THE THRONE.

THE LEGACY OF ANCIENT MESOPOTAMIA

MATHEMATICS

THERE ARE 60 SECONDS IN A MINUTE, 60 MINUTES IN AN HOUR, AND 12 HOURS ON A CLOCK.

The Babylonian people were very good mathematicians. They developed a type of mathematics called "sexagesimal", or the "base 60 system", from the ancient Sumerians. Historians believe that the Babylonians used 60 as their base number because it can easily be divided by many numbers including 12, 10, 6, and 5. These divisions can be seen on the face of a clock, where we still use base 60 today.

Nowadays, most people use ten as the base number of mathematics, a system called the decimal numeral system which is similar to the one used by the ancient Assyrians. This means that all numbers are represented by a *digit* between 0 and 9, and the positions of numbers (tens, hundreds, and thousands) are based on powers of ten. One example of base 10 being used today is in the *metric system*. There are ten millimeters in a centimeter, 100 centimeters in a meter, and 1,000 meters in a kilometer.

THE WHEEL

Before the wheel was invented, it was very difficult for people in the ancient world to transport heavy objects. They could use the nearby rivers to float things along, or roll them across the ground on top of logs. Both of these methods were quite slow and not very easy.

Some historians believe that the wheel was invented in Mesopotamia in around 3500 B.C. They carved wheels from thick tree trunks. The wheel was a very important invention and it has led to the powerful forms of transportation that can be seen today, such as bicycles, cars, and trains. At first, Mesopotamians used wheels when making pottery, on something called a potter's wheel. However, around 500 years later, they developed a type of vehicle called a chariot by attaching the wheel to an *axle*. The chariots were pulled by horses and were often used in battle, driven by someone called a charioteer.

5000 B.C.
PEOPLE FIRST SETTLE IN SUMER

TIMELINE OF

4500 B.C.
URUK IS FOUNDED BY THE SUMERIAN KING ENMERKAR

3100 B.C.

SUMERIAN LANGUAGE AND WRITING FIRST APPEARS IN MESOPOTAMIA

3000 B.C.

PEOPLE IN MESOPOTAMIA BEGIN BUILDING CHARIOTS

1900 B.C.

THE CITY OF ASHUR IS FOUNDED, AND THE ASSYRIAN EMPIRE BEGINS

1792 B.C.

HAMMURABI BECOMES THE KING OF BABYLON

689 B.C.

THE ASSYRIANS DESTROY BABYLON

612 B.C.

THE ASSYRIAN CITY OF NINEVEH IS CAPTURED BY THE BABYLONIANS AND THE MEDES PEOPLE

605-562 B.C.

NEBUCHADNEZZAR II IS THE KING OF BABYLON

ANCIENT MESOPOTAMIA

2334 B.C.

THE AKKADIANS OVERTHROW THE SUMERIAN CIVILIZATION

2144-2124 B.C.

GUDEA REIGNS AS THE LEADER OF THE SUMERIAN CITY OF LAGASH

2000 B.C.

EPIC TALE OF GILGAMESH IS FIRST RECORDED

575 B.C.

NEBUCHADNEZZAR II BUILDS THE ISHTAR GATE IN BABYLON

550 B.C.

CYRUS THE GREAT BECOMES LEADER OF THE ACHAEMENID EMPIRE

485 B.C.

XERXES I DESTROYS BABYLON

333 B.C.

ALEXANDER THE GREAT CONQUERS THE ACHAEMENID EMPIRE

A.D. 651

MUSLIM ARABS OVERTHROW THE SASANIAN EMPIRE

MAP OF ANCIENT MESOPOTAMIA

NINEVEH

ASHUR

TIGRIS RIVER

AKKAD

EUPHRATES RIVER

NIPPUR

BABYLON

LAGASH

URUK

UR

ERIDU

KEY
- BABYLONIAN CITIES
- ASSYRIAN CITIES
- AKKADIAN CITIES
- SUMERIAN CITIES

GLOSSARY

A.D.	meaning "in the year of the Lord", it marks the time after Christians believe Jesus was born
assault	a violent attack on someone that can be physical or verbal
axle	a bar on which a wheel turns
B.C.	meaning "before Christ", it is used to mark dates that occurred before Christians believe Jesus was born
ceremonies	formal occasions celebrating achievements, people, or religious or public events
chariots	two-wheeled vehicles, pulled by horses
civil war	fighting between different groups of people in the same country
civilizations	societies that are very advanced
communities	groups of people that live and work in the same area, and share similar values and beliefs
conquered	to have overcome or taken control of something by force
digit	any of the whole numbers between zero and nine
fertile	somewhere that plants and crops can be easily grown
governor	a person who leads a government
hierarchy	a system where people are ranked in order of power, status, or authority
influential	able to affect the behavior of someone or something
insulated	able to stop the movement of heat, electricity, or sound
kingdom	countries, states, or territories that are ruled by a king or queen
legend	famous; talked about in old, traditional stories
merchants	people involved in trading goods, often with other countries
metric system	a system of measuring and weighing things that is based on the number ten
offerings	gifts presented to gods during a religious ceremony
organized religion	a religion that has a set of rules and practices and a hierarchy of religious officials
permanent	(intended to) last forever
profession	a job that needs special training
reconstruction	something that has been rebuilt to look like the original
reign	the period of time that a leader rules
relief	a piece of art that has been carved out of a certain material to create raised images
rich	to have a large amount of something
scribes	people who write on behalf of someone else
slavery	the state of being owned by another person and having no freedom
social classes	groups of people who have the same social status and similar levels of wealth
stele	a tall stone pillar that is carved with writing or drawings and is found in or near important places like temples
thrive	to grow or develop successfully
tribes	groups of people linked together by family, society, religion, or community